CROCKPOT
FAMILY FAVORITES

STEP-by-STEP Recipes:
Cooking Deliciously is Easy !

Ariel MULLINS

Copyright © 2025 by Vertex Publishing

All rights reserved. No part of this publication may be reproduced, stored in a retrieval system, or transmitted in any form or by any means — electronic, mechanical, photocopying, recording, or otherwise — without the prior written permission of the publisher, except in the case of brief quotations embodied in critical articles or reviews.

Published by Vertex Publishing

Author

Ariel Mullins

Design & Layout

Victoria Nedbaeva

This book is intended for informational and entertainment purposes only. The publisher and the author disclaim any liability for any adverse effects or consequences from the use of any information, recipes, or suggestions contained herein.

Every effort has been made to ensure the accuracy of the content, but the results of the recipes may vary depending on individual cooking equipment, ingredient brands, interpretation, and environmental factors. Photographs are for illustrative purposes only and may not exactly represent the final appearance of the dishes prepared.

Always observe proper food safety practices, read appliance manuals carefully, and consult a healthcare provider regarding any dietary concerns or food allergies.

ISBN 979-8-9929659-1-9

Printed in the United States

Table of Contens

- Introduction 7
- Basics of the Multi-Cooker 8
- Common Mistakes and Useful Tips 9

Soups & Stews 11

- Slow Cooker Chipotle Beef Chili 12
- Slow Cooker Chicken Tortilla Soup 13
- Slow Cooker Potato Soup 14
- Slow Cooker Chili 15
- Slow Cooker Split Pea Soup 16
- Slow Cooker White Chicken Chili 17
- Slow Cooker Broccoli Cheese Soup 18
- Slow Cooker Beef Stew 19
- Slow Cooker Lasagna Soup 20
- Slow Cooker Cauliflower Corn Chowder 21
- Slow Cooker Turkey Chili 22
- Crockpot Tomato Soup 23
- Slow Cooker Creamy Tomato Basil Tortellini Soup 24
- Slow Cooker Mushroom Barley Stew 25

Chicken & Poultry 26

- Slow Cooker Chicken and Dumplings 27
- Slow Cooker BBQ Chicken 28
- Slow Cooker Chicken Lettuce Cups 29
- Slow Cooker Chicken Cacciatore 30
- Crockpot Chicken and Rice 31
- Crock Pot Chicken Drumsticks 32
- Slow Cooker Greek Chicken 33

Table of Contens

Slow Cooker Honey Garlic Chicken and Veggies 34
Slow Cooker Chicken and Mushroom Stroganoff 35
Slow Cooker Chicken Parmesan Pasta 36
Slow Cooker Chicken in Tomato and Herb Sauce 37
Slow Cooker Chicken Adobo 38
Crockpot Italian Chicken 39
Slow Cooker Sriracha Chili Chicken Wings 40

Beef & Pork 41

Slow Cooker Pulled Pork Tacos 42
Slow Cooker Pulled Pork 43
Slow Cooker Pot Roast 44
Slow-Cooker Drip Beef Sandwiches 45
Slow Cooker Brisket 46
Slow-Cooker Teriyaki Ribs 47
Slow Cooker Corned Beef and Cabbage 48
Slow Cooker Ham 49
Drip Beef with Sherry 50
Slow Cooker Pork Chops 51
Slow Cooker Hungarian Goulash & Noodles 52
Slow Cooker BBQ Pulled Beef 53
Slow Cooker Bolognese 54
Red Wine Braised Short Ribs 55
Slow Cooker Shepherd's Pie 56
Pressure Cooker Pot Roast 57

Table of Contens

Side Dishes & Vegetables 58
- Crock Pot Mac and Cheese 59
- Slow Cooker Green Beans with Bacon 60
- Crock Pot Stuffing 61
- Crock Pot Scalloped Potatoes 62
- Slow Cooker Mashed Potatoes 63
- Slow Cooker Refried Beans 64
- Slow Cooker Garlic Herb Mushrooms 65
- Slow Cooker Southern Collard Greens 66
- Slow Cooker Tater Tot Casserole 67
- Slow Cooker Honey Glazed Carrots 68

Appetizers & Dips 69
- Easy Queso Dip 70
- Cocktail Meatballs 71
- Crock Pot Buffalo Chicken Dip 72
- Beer Cheese Dip 73
- Shredded BBQ Chicken Nachos 74
- Crock Pot Swedish Meatballs 75

Desserts & Sweets 76
- Crock Pot Candy 77
- Slow Cooker Applesauce 78
- Homemade Apple Butter 79
- Slow Cooker Banana Bread Pudding 80

Table of Contens

Beverages 81
- **Crock Pot Hot Chocolate** 82
- **Mulled Wine** 83
- **Homemade Slow Cooker Apple Cider** 84
- **Slow Cooker Spiced Chai Tea** 85

Pasta & Casseroles 86
- **Crockpot Lasagna** 87
- **Slow Cooker Mexican Lasagna** 88

Measurement Conversion Chart 89

Thank you for your purchase! 90

Introduction

Welcome to your ultimate guide to multi-cooker mastery! Whether you're a busy professional, a parent juggling multiple responsibilities, or simply someone who appreciates the convenience of modern kitchen technology, this cookbook is designed to transform your culinary experience.

The multi-cooker has revolutionized home cooking by combining multiple appliances into one versatile device. With the ability to pressure cook, slow cook, sauté, steam, and more, this kitchen marvel allows you to create delicious, nutritious meals with minimal effort and maximum flavor. Gone are the days of watching over multiple pots and pans — your multi-cooker can handle everything from hearty stews to delicate desserts with just the press of a button.

In this Cookbook, we've compiled a diverse collection of recipes spanning from protein-packed main courses to indulgent desserts, all optimized for your multi-cooker. Each recipe has been carefully tested to ensure perfect results every time, regardless of your cooking experience. Beyond recipes, we've included a comprehensive four-week meal plan to help you incorporate your multi-cooker into daily life, along with storage tips to make the most of your culinary creations.

Our goal is simple: to help you discover the joy of effortless cooking while creating memorable meals for yourself and your loved ones. So plug in your multi-cooker, turn these pages, and embark on a delicious journey of culinary convenience!

Basics of the Multi-Cooker

Understanding Your Device

The modern multi-cooker is a technological marvel that combines numerous cooking functions in one compact appliance. Most models offer these essential functions:

- **Pressure Cooking:** Uses steam pressure to cook food quickly while locking in flavors and nutrients
- **Slow Cooking**: Gently cooks food at low temperatures over several hours
- **Sautéing/Browning**: Allows you to sear meats or sauté vegetables directly in the cooking pot
- **Steaming**: Cooks food using hot steam, preserving nutrients and texture
- **Rice Cooking**: Perfectly prepares various types of rice and grains
- **Yogurt Making**: Maintains the precise temperature needed for yogurt fermentation
- **Keep Warm**: Holds food at serving temperature without overcooking

Essential Parts and Components

Familiarize yourself with these key components of your multi-cooker:

- **Inner Pot**: The removable cooking vessel, typically made of stainless steel or non-stick material
- **Lid**: Features a sealing ring and pressure release valve
- **Control Panel**: Digital interface for selecting cooking functions and times
- **Steam Release Valve**: Allows you to release pressure naturally or manually
- **Condensation Collector**: Catches excess moisture during cooking
- **Sealing Ring**: Creates the airtight seal necessary for pressure cooking
- **Accessories**: May include a steamer basket, rice paddle, measuring cup, and recipe booklet

Safety First

Before cooking with your multi-cooker, always:

- Ensure the sealing ring is properly installed and free from damage
- Check that the steam release valve is clean and functioning correctly
- Keep your face and hands away from the steam release valve when releasing pressure
- Use sufficient liquid (at least 1 cup) when pressure cooking
- Never fill the pot beyond the maximum fill line (typically 2/3 full)

Common Mistakes and Useful Tips

Common Mistakes to Avoid

1. **Insufficient Liquid:** Always use at least 1 cup of liquid when pressure cooking to create adequate steam.

2. **Overfilling:** Never fill your multi-cooker beyond the maximum fill line, especially when cooking foods that expand (like rice or beans).

3. **Forgetting to Seal:** Ensure the pressure release valve is in the "sealed" position before pressure cooking.

4. **Releasing Pressure Incorrectly:** Stand clear of the steam release valve when performing a quick release to avoid burns.

5. **Cooking Dairy Under Pressure:** Milk and cream can curdle under pressure—add these ingredients after pressure cooking is complete.

6. **Ignoring Natural Release Times:** Some recipes require a natural pressure release to prevent food from becoming overcooked or splattering.

7. **Storing with Lid Sealed:** Always store your multi-cooker with the lid resting upside down to prevent odors and mold growth.

8. **Neglecting the Sealing Ring:** The silicone ring absorbs odors over time; clean thoroughly or keep separate rings for sweet and savory dishes.

Pro Tips for Multi-Cooker Success

➪ **Layer Ingredients Strategically**: Place longer-cooking items at the bottom and quicker-cooking items on top.

➪ **Use the Sauté Function First**: Brown meats and sauté aromatics before pressure cooking to develop deeper flavors.

➪ **Adjust Cooking Times for Altitude**: If you live at high altitude, increase cooking time by 5% for every 1,000 feet above 2,000 feet.

➪ **Convert Slow Cooker Recipes**: Most slow cooker recipes can be adapted for the pressure cooker function by reducing liquid by 1/3 and drastically cutting cooking time.

➪ **Thicken After Cooking**: Cornstarch slurries or flour mixtures should be added after pressure cooking to prevent scorching.

➪ **Use Pot-in-Pot Method**: For delicate dishes or to cook multiple items simultaneously, use the pot-in-pot technique with a heat-safe bowl on a trivet.

➪ **Prep Ingredients in Advance**: Having everything ready before you start cooking makes the process smoother and more enjoyable.

➪ **Keep a Cooking Journal**: Record your adjustments and results to perfect your favorite recipes over time.

Soups & Stews

Slow Cooker Chipotle Beef Chili

Prep Time:
1 hour

Cook Time:
8 hours

Servings:
4-6

Ingredients:

- 6 slices thick-cut bacon, cut into pieces
- 3 lbs boneless beef chuck, cubed
- 2 onions, chopped
- 4 garlic cloves, chopped
- 2 tsp dried oregano
- 1 Tbsp ground cumin
- 2 chipotle chiles in adobo, chopped
- 2 Tbsp adobo sauce
- 2 Tbsp dark brown sugar
- 4 cups low-sodium beef broth
- 2 tsp kosher salt
- 1/4 cup masa harina

Instructions:

1. **Cook the bacon.** Cook bacon until browned (6-8 minutes). Remove. Cook beef in the same fat until browned (6-8 minutes). Remove.

2. **Prepare vegetables and spices.** Cook onions and garlic (3-4 minutes). Add oregano and cumin, cook 1 minute. Deglaze with 1/4 cup water.

3. **Slow cook.** Transfer all ingredients to slow cooker. Add chipotles, adobo sauce, sugar and broth. Season. Cook on high for 4 hours or low for 8 hours.

4. **Thicken and serve.** When chili is done, mix masa harina with 1/4 cup water and add to chili. Serve with sour cream, sliced scallions, and corn chips.

Slow Cooker Chicken Tortilla Soup

Prep Time: 10 mins

Cook Time: 5 hours

Servings: 12

Ingredients:

- 3 chicken breasts
- 2 tsp chili powder
- 1 tsp cumin
- Salt and pepper, to taste
- 1 medium onion, chopped
- 1 red bell pepper, chopped
- 1 yellow bell pepper, chopped
- 1 (28-oz) can tomatoes, with juice
- 1 (10-oz) can diced tomatoes and green chilies
- 3 cups low sodium chicken broth
- 1 (15-oz) can black beans, drained and rinsed
- 1 whole chipotle pepper in adobo
- 4 oz tomato paste
- 1 lime, juiced

Instructions:

1. **Prepare chicken.** Place chicken in slow cooker. Season with chili powder, cumin, salt, and pepper.
2. **Combine ingredients.** Add onion, bell peppers, tomatoes, tomatoes with green chilies, broth, tomato paste, chipotle pepper, and black beans. Stir.
3. **Cook.** Cover and cook on high for 5 hours (or low for 8 hours).
4. **Finish soup.** Stir in lime juice. Shred chicken using two forks. Adjust seasoning if needed.
5. **Serve.** Top with sour cream, avocado, cilantro, cheese, and crushed tortilla chips.

Slow Cooker Potato Soup

Prep Time: 20 mins

Cook Time: 4 hrs

Servings: 6-8

Ingredients:

- 6 slices bacon, chopped
- 2 lbs russet potatoes, peeled and cubed
- 3 celery stalks, sliced
- 1 large leek, cleaned and chopped
- 3 garlic cloves, finely chopped
- 4 cups chicken stock
- 1 tsp kosher salt
- 6 sprigs fresh thyme
- 1/2 tsp ground black pepper
- 3/4 cup sour cream, plus more for serving

Instructions:

1. **Cook bacon.** Heat skillet over medium heat. Cook bacon until golden (6-8 minutes). Reserve 2 pieces for garnish and crumble the rest.

2. **Combine ingredients.** Place crumbled bacon, potatoes, celery, leek, garlic, stock, salt, thyme sprigs, and pepper in slow cooker.

3. **Cook.** Cover and cook on high for 4 hours (or low for 6-8 hours) until potatoes are tender.

4. **Blend soup.** Remove thyme sprigs. Blend to semi-smooth consistency, leaving small chunks for texture.

5. **Finish and serve.** Stir in sour cream. Adjust consistency with water if needed. Serve topped with cheese, chives, sour cream, and reserved bacon.

Slow Cooker Chili

Prep Time: 20 mins

Cook Time: 4 hrs 20 mins

Servings: 6-8

Ingredients:

- 1 Tbsp vegetable oil
- 1 yellow onion, chopped
- 1 green bell pepper, chopped
- 2 lbs ground beef
- 4 garlic cloves, chopped
- 2 Tbsp chili powder
- 1 Tbsp ground cumin
- 2 tsp dried oregano
- 1 (28-oz) can diced tomatoes
- 1 (8-oz) can tomato sauce
- 3 (15-oz) cans kidney beans, drained and rinsed
- 1 (14-oz) can beef broth
- 1 chipotle chile in adobo
- 2 Tbsp adobo sauce
- 1 1/2 tsp salt
- 1 tsp ground black pepper

Instructions:

1. **Sauté vegetables.** Heat oil over medium-high heat. Add onion and bell pepper, cook until softened (5-7 minutes).

2. **Cook beef.** Add ground beef and break apart. Cook until no longer pink (6-8 minutes). Add garlic and cook 1 more minute. Drain mixture.

3. **Combine in slow cooker.** Transfer beef mixture to slow cooker. Add chili powder, cumin, oregano, tomatoes, tomato sauce, kidney beans, beef broth, chipotle, adobo sauce, salt, and pepper. Stir.

4. **Cook.** Cover and cook on high for 4 hours or low for 6 hours.

5. **Serve.** Reduce to warm setting and serve topped with sour cream, cheese, jalapeños, and tortilla chips.

Slow Cooker Split Pea Soup

Prep Time:
10 mins

Cook Time:
4-5 hrs (high) or
8-10 hrs (low)

Servings:
6-8

Ingredients:

- 1 lb dried split green peas
- 1/2 onion, chopped
- 3 carrots, peeled and sliced
- 2 pieces of celery, sliced
- 2 cloves garlic, chopped
- 8 oz cubed ham
- 1 qt chicken stock
- 1 1/2 cups water
- 4 sprigs fresh thyme
- 2 sprigs parsley
- 1 bay leaf (optional)
- Salt and pepper, to taste

Instructions:

1. **Prepare peas.** Place peas in a colander. Rinse well and pick through for pebbles or debris.

2. **Combine ingredients.** In slow cooker, combine peas, onion, carrots, celery, garlic, ham, chicken stock and water.

3. **Add herbs.** Tie thyme, parsley and bay leaf together with kitchen twine and add to slow cooker.

4. **Cook.** Cover and cook on high for 4-5 hours or low for 8-10 hours, until peas are tender and have split to thicken the soup.

5. **Season and serve.** Season with salt and pepper to taste. Serve topped with chopped parsley.

Slow Cooker White Chicken Chili

Prep Time: 20 mins

Cook Time: 7 hrs 50 mins

Servings: 4-6

Ingredients:

- 3 skinless, boneless chicken breasts (about 1 1/2 pounds)
- 1 Tbsp ground cumin
- 1 Tbsp ground coriander
- 2 tsp dried oregano
- 1/2 tsp paprika
- 1/2 tsp crushed red pepper flakes
- 1 (10-oz) bag frozen corn
- Black pepper, to taste
- 2 (15-oz) cans cannellini beans, drained and rinsed
- 2 (4-oz) cans chopped green chiles
- 2 garlic cloves, minced
- 2 cups low-sodium chicken broth
- 1/2 cup heavy cream
- 2 Tbsp masa harina
- 1 tsp kosher salt

Instructions:

1. **Prepare chicken.** Place chicken in slow cooker. Mix spices in small bowl and sprinkle over chicken.
2. **Add ingredients.** Add beans, green chiles, garlic, and chicken broth. Stir to combine.
3. **Cook.** Cover and cook on low for 7-8 hours, until chicken is cooked through.
4. **Shred chicken.** Remove chicken and shred with two forks.
5. **Thicken and finish.** Combine heavy cream and masa harina until smooth. Return chicken to slow cooker. Add masa mixture and corn. Cook 30 more minutes until thickened.
6. **Serve.** Top with cheese and avocado. Garnish with lime wedges.

Slow Cooker Broccoli Cheese Soup

Prep Time: 5 mins

Cook Time: 4 hrs 5 mins

Servings: 12

Ingredients:

- 1 lb frozen broccoli florets
- 1 medium onion, diced
- 2 carrots, finely diced
- 5 cups low sodium chicken broth
- 2 cans cream of celery soup
- 1/4 tsp seasoned salt
- 1/4 tsp salt (plus more to taste)
- 1/2 tsp black pepper
- 1/8 tsp cayenne pepper
- 1 1/2 lb Velveeta
- 2 cups grated sharp cheddar cheese

Instructions:

1. **Combine ingredients.** Add broccoli, onion, carrots, chicken broth, cream of celery soup, and all seasonings to slow cooker.
2. **Cook.** Stir ingredients and set to high for 4 hours.
3. **Blend.** Use an immersion blender to puree 3/4 of the soup. (If using regular blender, blend only 1 cup at a time with caution.)
4. **Add cheese.** Add Velveeta and cheddar. Turn to low and cover for 15 minutes.
5. **Finish and serve.** Stir to melt cheese completely. Adjust seasoning if needed. Serve garnished with additional cheese or crumbled crackers if desired.

Slow Cooker Beef Stew

Prep Time: 10 mins

Cook Time: 4 hrs 10 mins

Servings: 6-8

Ingredients:

- 2 1/2 lbs beef stew meat
- 1 1/2 cups beef stock
- 3/4 cup red wine
- 3 Tbsp tomato paste
- 3 Tbsp Worcestershire sauce
- 1/4 cup all-purpose flour
- 3 cloves garlic, chopped
- 1 1/2 tsp seasoned salt
- 1/2 tsp ground black pepper (plus more to taste)
- 4 sprigs thyme
- 1 onion, cut into 1-inch pieces
- 3 carrots, cut into 1-inch pieces
- 3 stalks celery, cut into 1-inch pieces
- 8 oz whole mushrooms, halved

Instructions:

1. **Prepare base.** Place beef in slow cooker. Whisk together beef stock, wine, tomato paste, Worcestershire sauce, flour, garlic, salt, and pepper.

2. **Add liquid and vegetables.** Pour liquid over beef. Add thyme sprigs, then layer onion, carrot, celery, and mushrooms on top.

3. **Cook.** Cover and cook on high for 4-5 hours, stirring halfway through.

4. **Finish and serve.** Remove thyme sprigs. Season with additional salt and pepper to taste. Serve over egg noodles or mashed potatoes. Sprinkle with fresh parsley.

Slow Cooker Lasagna Soup

Prep Time: 20 mins

Cook Time: 3 hrs

Servings: 8

Instructions:

1. **Heat** olive oil in a non-stick skillet over medium heat. Sauté onion, garlic, and mushrooms until softened, 4-5 minutes.

2. **Transfer** sautéed mixture to a 6-quart slow cooker. Add zucchini, crushed tomatoes, tomato paste, vegetable broth, bay leaves, basil, oregano, red pepper flakes, salt, and pepper.

3. **Cook** on low for 7 hours or on high for 3 hours.

4. **Prepare** lasagna noodles separately according to package directions. Drain and cut into smaller pieces.

5. **Add** cooked noodles and spinach to the slow cooker. Mix ricotta, mozzarella, parsley, basil, and salt in a small bowl. Stir half the cheese mixture into the soup and serve with remaining cheese on top.

Ingredients:

- 1 Tbsp extra virgin olive oil
- 1 medium yellow onion, diced
- 4 cloves garlic, minced
- 2 cups brown mushrooms, sliced
- 2 zucchinis, sliced
- 1 (28-oz) can crushed tomatoes
- 3 Tbsp tomato paste
- 4 cups vegetable broth
- 2 bay leaves
- 2 tsp dried basil
- 2 tsp dried oregano
- 1/8 tsp red pepper flakes
- 2 tsp kosher salt
- 2 tsp freshly ground black pepper
- 6 oz lasagna noodles
- 4 cups fresh spinach
- 8 oz ricotta cheese
- 1 cup mozzarella cheese, shredded
- 1/4 cup parsley, chopped
- 1/4 cup fresh basil leaves, chopped
- Pinch of kosher salt

Slow Cooker Cauliflower Corn Chowder

Prep Time: 30 mins

Cook Time: 3 hrs 30 mins

Servings: 6

Ingredients:

- 1 cup yellow onion, finely chopped
- 3/4 cup celery, diced
- 3/4 cup carrot, diced
- 1 tsp olive oil
- 1/8 tsp cayenne pepper
- 1 tsp fresh thyme, chopped
- 3 cups cauliflower florets, small pieces
- 3 cups corn, canned and drained
- 3 cups unsalted chicken stock
- 1 lb boneless skinless chicken breast
- 1 lb red potatoes, cut into 1/2-inch cubes
- 1 cup whole milk
- 3/4 tsp kosher salt
- 1 bay leaf
- 2 Tbsp minced parsley
- Bacon
- Sautéed cauliflower florets

Instructions:

1. **Microwave** onions, celery, carrots, olive oil, cayenne pepper, and thyme for 3 minutes. Stir, then microwave another 3 minutes. Transfer to slow cooker.

2. **Blend** cauliflower florets (microwaved with 1/4 cup water for 5 minutes) with 1 1/2 cups corn and 2 cups chicken stock until smooth.

3. **Combine** blended mixture, remaining stock, chicken breasts, potatoes, milk, salt, and bay leaf in slow cooker. Cook on High for 3-4 hours or Low for 5-6 hours.

4. **Remove** bay leaf and shred chicken. Stir in remaining corn and heat for 10 minutes.

5. **Serve** hot with parsley and optional toppings.

Slow Cooker Turkey Chili

Prep Time:
15 mins

Cook Time:
4 hrs 15 mins

Servings:
6-8

Instructions:

1. **Heat** oil in a large skillet over medium-high heat. Cook onion and bell pepper until tender, 8-10 minutes.

2. **Add** ground turkey and cook until no longer pink, 6-8 minutes. Then add garlic and tomato paste, cook for 2 minutes.

3. **Transfer** turkey mixture to slow cooker. Stir in tomatoes, beans, corn, broth, and all seasonings.

4. **Cook** on high for 4 hours or low for 6 hours.

5. **Serve** warm with optional garnishes.

Ingredients:

- 1 Tbsp vegetable oil
- 1 yellow onion, chopped
- 1 red bell pepper, chopped
- 2 lbs ground turkey
- 3 garlic cloves, chopped
- 1/4 cup tomato paste
- 2 (14.5-oz) cans fire-roasted tomatoes
- 1 (15-oz) can black beans, drained and rinsed
- 1 1/2 cups chicken broth
- 2 tsp chili powder
- 1 (15-oz) can kidney beans, drained and rinsed
- 1 cup frozen corn kernels
- 1 tsp ground cumin
- 1 tsp dried oregano
- 1/2 tsp salt
- 1/2 tsp ground black pepper
- Shredded pepper jack cheese
- Diced avocado
- Corn chips

Crockpot Tomato Soup

Prep Time: 10 mins

Cook Time: 5 hrs 45 mins

Servings: 6

Ingredients:

- 1 Tbsp extra-virgin olive oil
- 2 medium yellow onions, chopped (about 3 cups)
- 3 cloves garlic, minced
- 1 (28-oz) can whole plum tomatoes with juices
- 3 cups reduced-sodium chicken or vegetable broth
- 2 tsp kosher salt
- 1 tsp hot Hungarian paprika
- 1/2 tsp ground black pepper
- 1/3 cup whole wheat orzo
- 1/4 cup half-and-half (optional)
- Freshly grated Parmesan cheese
- Chopped fresh basil or parsley

Instructions:

1. **Sauté** onions in olive oil for 15 minutes until golden brown. Add garlic and cook for 1 more minute.
2. **Combine** sautéed vegetables, tomatoes, broth, salt, paprika, and pepper in slow cooker. Cook on low for 5-6 hours or high for 2-3 hours.
3. **Purée** soup until smooth using an immersion blender or regular blender.
4. **Add** orzo, increase heat to high, and cook uncovered for 20-30 minutes until tender. Stir in half-and-half if using.
5. **Serve** hot with Parmesan and fresh herbs as desired.

Slow Cooker Creamy Tomato Basil Tortellini Soup

Prep Time: 15 mins

Cook Time: 6 hrs 45 mins

Servings: 7

Ingredients:

- 1 3/4 cups diced carrots (3 medium)
- 1 3/4 cups diced yellow onion (1 large)
- 2 Tbsp olive oil
- 5 cloves garlic, minced
- 3 (28-oz) cans whole Roma tomatoes
- 1 (32-oz) carton vegetable broth
- 1/3 cup chopped fresh basil, plus more for garnish
- 2 bay leaves
- 1 Tbsp granulated sugar
- Salt and freshly ground black pepper, to taste
- 16 oz refrigerated three-cheese tortellini
- 3/4 cup heavy cream
- Shredded Parmesan, for serving

Instructions:

1. **Sauté** carrots and onion in olive oil for 3-4 minutes. Add garlic and sauté 1 minute longer, then transfer to slow cooker.
2. **Combine** with tomatoes, broth, basil, bay leaves, sugar, salt and pepper. Cook on LOW for 6-7 hours or HIGH for 3-3.5 hours.
3. **Purée** the soup after removing bay leaves.
4. **Add** tortellini, cover, and cook on HIGH for 15-20 minutes until heated through.
5. **Stir** in heavy cream and serve topped with Parmesan cheese and fresh basil.

Slow Cooker Mushroom Barley Stew

Prep Time: 10 mins

Cook Time: 6 hrs 10 mins

Servings: 8

Instructions:

1. **Combine** all ingredients except salt, pepper, parsley and bread in slow cooker.
2. **Cook** on low heat for 6-8 hours.
3. **Remove** bay leaf when cooking is complete.
4. **Season** with kosher salt and black pepper to taste.
5. **Serve** in bowls with fresh parsley and warm crusty bread if desired.

Ingredients:

- 1 (15-oz) can fire-roasted diced tomatoes
- 2 medium rutabagas, diced large
- 2 medium carrots, sliced
- 2 short stalks celery, sliced
- 1 leek or 1 yellow onion, diced
- 1 lb cremini mushrooms, quartered
- 1 cup uncooked barley
- 8 cups vegetable stock or broth
- 1 bay leaf
- Kosher salt, to taste
- Freshly ground black pepper, to taste
- Fresh parsley, for garnish (optional)
- Crusty bread, for serving (optional)

Chicken & Poultry

Slow Cooker Chicken and Dumplings

Prep Time: 30 mins

Cook Time: 4-5 hrs

Servings: 8-12

Ingredients:

- 4 garlic cloves, minced
- 3 stalks celery, thinly sliced
- 2 medium carrots, thinly sliced
- 1 large yellow onion, sliced
- 2 (10.5-oz) cans cream of chicken soup
- 2 (10.5-oz) cans cream of mushroom soup
- 2 1/2 cups chicken broth
- 1 1/2 lbs boneless skinless chicken thighs
- 1 cup frozen peas
- 1 (6-oz) can buttermilk biscuits
- 1 cup white cheddar cheese, grated
- 2 Tbsp minced fresh chives
- Chopped parsley, for serving

Instructions:

1. **Place** garlic, celery, carrots, and onion in the bottom of a 6-8 quart slow cooker. Add soups and broth, whisk to combine.

2. **Add** chicken, cover, and cook on low for 4-5 hours, or on high for 3-4 hours until tender.

3. **Remove** chicken, shred with a fork, and return to slow cooker with frozen peas.

4. **Prepare** biscuits by sprinkling with cheddar cheese and chives, cut into quarters and place on top of soup.

5. **Cook** for 30-45 minutes on high until biscuits are cooked through. Let stand 10-15 minutes before serving.

Slow Cooker BBQ Chicken

Prep Time:
5 mins

Cook Time:
2 hrs 35 mins

Servings:
6-8

Ingredients:

- 1 1/2 cups BBQ sauce
- 2 Tbsp apple cider vinegar (plus more to taste)
- 2 Tbsp packed light brown sugar
- 1 tsp paprika
- 1/2 tsp kosher salt (plus more to taste)
- 1/2 tsp ground black pepper
- 1/4 tsp ground cayenne pepper
- 4 garlic cloves, crushed
- 1/2 medium yellow onion, thinly sliced
- 3 lbs boneless, skinless chicken thighs or breasts

Instructions:

1. **Whisk** together BBQ sauce, vinegar, brown sugar, spices, garlic, and onion in a 6-8 quart slow cooker.
2. **Add** chicken, stirring to ensure it is fully coated with sauce.
3. **Cook** on low for 4-6 hours or on high for 2-3 hours until chicken is tender and shreds easily.
4. **Shred** chicken using two forks and return to sauce. Cook on low for 30 additional minutes.
5. **Adjust** seasoning with additional salt or vinegar if needed before serving.

Slow Cooker Chicken Lettuce Cups

Prep Time: 20 mins

Cook Time: 4 hrs 20 mins

Servings: 8

Ingredients:

- 2 Tbsp fresh ginger
- 3 cloves garlic
- 1/4 cup low-sodium tamari (gluten-free soy sauce)
- 1/4 cup gluten-free hoisin sauce
- 1/4 cup rice vinegar
- 3 Tbsp sesame oil
- 1 Fresno chili
- 2 Tbsp honey
- 2 1/2 lbs skinless chicken breasts, bone-in
- 1 red onion, julienned
- 1 orange, quartered
- 1 cup water chestnuts, chopped
- 1 cup sliced green onions, divided
- 1 Tbsp toasted sesame seeds
- Kosher salt to taste
- 1 red or yellow bell pepper, diced
- 1 red Fresno chili, thinly sliced
- 1 head butter lettuce, leaves separated
- 1 cup cucumber slices
- 1/3 cup fresh mint leaves
- 1/3 cup fresh Thai basil leaves
- 1/3 cup fresh cilantro leaves

Instructions:

1. **Blend** sauce ingredients until smooth. Place chicken, red onion, and orange in slow cooker and pour sauce over.
2. **Cook** on high for 4 hours, adding water chestnuts with 1 hour left.
3. **Shred** chicken, discarding skin and bones, and season with salt.
4. **Mix** shredded chicken with 1/2 cup green onions and sesame seeds.
5. **Serve** with lettuce leaves, cucumber, herbs, and remaining vegetables for assembly.

Slow Cooker Chicken Cacciatore

Prep Time:
20 mins

Cook Time:
4 hrs 20 mins

Servings:
8-10

Ingredients:

- 10 bone-in skinless chicken thighs (about 5 oz each), trimmed
- Kosher salt and freshly ground black pepper
- Cooking spray or extra virgin olive oil
- 5 garlic cloves, finely chopped
- 1/2 large yellow onion, chopped
- 1 (28-oz) can crushed tomatoes
- 1/2 medium green bell pepper, chopped
- 1/2 medium red bell pepper, chopped
- 8 oz shiitake mushrooms, sliced
- 2 sprigs fresh thyme
- Fresh parsley for garnish
    - 2 bay leaves
    - Grated Parmesan cheese

Instructions:

1. **Brown** seasoned chicken in a skillet, 3-4 minutes per side, then transfer to slow cooker.
2. **Sauté** garlic and onion until soft, 3-4 minutes, and add to slow cooker with remaining ingredients.
3. **Cook** on high for 4 hours or low for 8 hours.
4. **Shred** chicken, discarding bones, and return to sauce.
5. **Serve** over pasta, polenta, or spaghetti squash, topped with Parmesan cheese.

Crockpot Chicken and Rice

Prep Time: 10 mins

Cook Time: 2 hrs 40 mins

Servings: 4

Ingredients:

- 1 cup long-grain brown rice
- 4 1/2 to 5 1/2 cups low-sodium chicken broth
- 1 1/2 cups diced carrots
- 1 small shallot, finely chopped
- 1 Tbsp Dijon mustard
- 1 1/2 lbs boneless, skinless chicken breasts
- 1 1/2 tsp garlic powder
- 1 tsp dried thyme
- 1/2 tsp kosher salt
- 1/4 tsp ground black pepper
- 1 cup frozen peas
- 1/2 cup nonfat plain Greek yogurt
- 1/2 cup freshly grated sharp cheddar cheese
- Chopped fresh parsley (optional)

Instructions:

1. **Prepare** rice by rinsing thoroughly and parboiling in 2 cups broth for 10 minutes, then drain.
2. **Combine** rice, carrots, shallot, and Dijon in slow cooker. Place chicken on top, season, and add 2 1/2 cups broth.
3. **Cook** on HIGH for 1 1/2 to 2 hours until chicken is cooked through. Remove chicken and continue cooking rice.
4. **Add** peas, yogurt, and diced chicken back to cooker. Stir in 1/4 cup cheese and sprinkle remainder on top.
5. **Heat** until cheese melts and serve garnished with parsley if desired.

Crock Pot Chicken Drumsticks

Prep Time:
10 mins

Cook Time:
4 hrs 10 mins

Servings:
4

Ingredients:

- 2 lbs chicken drumsticks
- Salt and pepper
- 2 Tbsp vegetable oil
- 2 1/2 cups BBQ sauce
- 1 cup honey
- 2 Tbsp cornstarch
- Fresh parsley for garnish

Instructions:

1. **Pat** chicken dry and season with salt and pepper. Brown in oil about 1 minute per side.
2. **Whisk** BBQ sauce and honey together and pour some in the bottom of greased slow cooker.
3. **Add** chicken and cover with remaining sauce. Cook on low for 4 hours or until chicken reaches 165°F.
4. **Make** a slurry with cornstarch and 2 Tbsp hot water. Add to sauce and cook 5 more minutes to thicken.
5. **Serve** with optional broiling for 5 minutes to crisp skin if desired.

Slow Cooker Greek Chicken

Prep Time: 15 mins

Cook Time: 3-4 hrs

Servings: 3-4

Ingredients:

- 3-4 boneless skinless chicken breasts (about 1 1/2 lbs)
- 1/4 cup extra-virgin olive oil
- 6 garlic cloves, minced
- 2 lemons (zest and juice)
- 1 tsp dried thyme
- 1 tsp dried oregano
- 1 1/2 tsp kosher salt
- 1/2 tsp ground black pepper
- 1 pint cherry tomatoes
- 1 large red onion, cut into 1/2-inch slices
- 1/2 cup pitted kalamata olives
- 1/2 cup crumbled feta cheese
- Fresh parsley for garnish

Instructions:

1. **Whisk** olive oil, garlic, lemon zest and juice, herbs, salt, and pepper. Marinate chicken for 30 minutes to 2 hours.

2. **Place** chicken in greased slow cooker with cherry tomatoes and red onion slices. Pour remaining marinade over top.

3. **Cook** on LOW for 3-4 hours or HIGH for 2-3 hours until chicken reaches 165°F.

4. **Add** kalamata olives during the last 30 minutes of cooking.

5. **Serve** topped with feta cheese and fresh parsley.

Slow Cooker Honey Garlic Chicken and Veggies

Prep Time: 10 mins

Cook Time: 8 hrs 15 mins

Servings: 4

Ingredients:

- 1/2 cup reduced sodium soy sauce
- 1/2 cup honey
- 1/4 cup ketchup
- 2 cloves garlic, minced
- 1 tsp dried basil
- 1/2 tsp dried oregano
- 1/4 tsp crushed red pepper flakes
- 1/4 tsp ground black pepper
- 8 bone-in, skin-on chicken thighs
- 16 oz baby red potatoes, halved
- 16 oz baby carrots
- 16 oz green beans, trimmed
- 2 Tbsp chopped fresh parsley leaves

Instructions:

1. **Combine** soy sauce, honey, ketchup, garlic, and seasonings in a large bowl.
2. **Place** chicken thighs and potatoes in slow cooker and pour sauce mixture over them.
3. **Cook** on LOW for 7-8 hours or HIGH for 3-4 hours, basting every hour.
4. **Add** green beans during the last 30 minutes of cooking.
5. **Serve** garnished with fresh parsley, optionally broiling chicken for 3-4 minutes for crispy skin.

Slow Cooker Chicken and Mushroom Stroganoff

Prep Time: 5 mins

Cook Time: 5 hrs 5 mins

Servings: 4

Ingredients:

- 4 boneless skinless chicken breasts, cubed
- 8 oz sliced mushrooms
- 8 oz cream cheese, softened
- 1 (10 1/2 oz) can cream of chicken soup
- 1 envelope (1 1/4 oz) dry onion soup mix
- Salt and pepper to taste
- Fresh parsley, chopped (for garnish)
- 8 oz large egg noodles (for serving)

Instructions:

1. **Place** chicken in greased slow cooker with mushrooms on top.
2. **Mix** cream cheese, cream of chicken soup, and dry onion soup mix until well combined and spread over chicken.
3. **Cook** on LOW for 4-6 hours or HIGH for 3 hours.
4. **Prepare** egg noodles according to package instructions.
5. **Serve** stroganoff over noodles, garnished with fresh chopped parsley.

Slow Cooker Chicken Parmesan Pasta

Prep Time: 15 mins

Cook Time: 4 hrs 45 mins

Servings: 8

Ingredients:

- 4 boneless skinless chicken breasts
- Kosher salt and freshly ground black pepper
- 2 (28-oz) cans crushed tomatoes
- 1 onion, diced
- 1 Tbsp dried basil
- 1 tsp dried oregano
- 1 tsp dried parsley
- 1/2 tsp crushed red pepper flakes (optional)
- 1 lb penne pasta
- 1 1/2 cups shredded mozzarella cheese
- 1/4 cup freshly grated Parmesan cheese
- 2 Tbsp chopped fresh parsley leaves

Instructions:

1. **Season** chicken with salt and pepper and place in slow cooker.
2. **Combine** crushed tomatoes, onion, and seasonings and pour over chicken. Cook on low for 4 hours.
3. **Remove** chicken and shred using two forks.
4. **Cook** pasta according to package instructions and add to slow cooker with shredded chicken.
5. **Top** with cheeses, cover, and cook 10-20 minutes until cheese melts. Garnish with fresh parsley.

Slow Cooker Chicken in Tomato and Herb Sauce

Prep Time: 15 mins

Cook Time: 3 hrs 10 mins

Servings: 8

Ingredients:

- 4 chicken breasts (halved lengthwise)
- 1 tbsp dried oregano
- 1 tbsp salt (plus more to taste)
- 2 tsp black pepper
- 8 oz white mushrooms, sliced
- 2 bell peppers, sliced
- 1/2 white onion
- 28 oz canned crushed tomatoes
- 2 tbsp tomato paste
- 1/2 cup red wine
- 5-6 garlic cloves
- 1 tbsp sugar
- 2-3 sprigs fresh thyme
- Vegetable oil for searing
- Pasta (for serving)
- Fresh parsley (optional, for garnish)

Instructions:

1. **Season** chicken with oregano, salt, and pepper mixture. Sear in oil for 1-2 minutes per side.
2. **Combine** tomatoes, paste, wine, garlic, and sugar in slow cooker. Add chicken, vegetables, and thyme.
3. **Cook** on high for 3 hours.
4. **Season** with salt to taste and discard thyme sprigs.
5. **Serve** over pasta with plenty of sauce.

37

Slow Cooker Chicken Adobo

Prep Time: 15 mins

Cook Time: 6-8 hrs

Servings: 4-6

Ingredients:

- 6-8 chicken thighs or drumsticks
- 1/2 cup soy sauce
- 1/2 cup white vinegar
- 1/4 cup water
- 1 whole head of garlic, cloves peeled and crushed
- 2-3 bay leaves
- 1 tsp whole black peppercorns
- 1 tbsp brown sugar
- 2 tbsp vegetable oil
- Black pepper to taste
- Steamed white rice
- Chopped green onions (optional)

Instructions:

1. **Mix** soy sauce, vinegar, water, and brown sugar. Season chicken with pepper and sear in oil until golden.

2. **Transfer** chicken to slow cooker with garlic, bay leaves, and peppercorns. Pour sauce mixture over chicken.

3. **Cook** on low for 6-8 hours or high for 3-4 hours until tender.

4. **Remove** chicken and optionally reduce sauce on stovetop for a few minutes.

5. **Serve** hot with steamed rice.

Crockpot Italian Chicken

Prep Time: 10 mins

Cook Time: 1.5-2.5 hrs

Servings: 4

Ingredients:

- 2 pounds boneless skinless chicken breasts
- 2 tablespoons extra virgin olive oil
- 1/2 teaspoon kosher salt
- 1/2 teaspoon freshly cracked black pepper
- 1 can (14 ounces) diced tomatoes
- 1/2 cup balsamic vinegar
- 3 cloves garlic, minced
- 1 bay leaf
- 1 teaspoon dried basil
- 1 small red onion, diced
- Shredded mozzarella cheese
- Fresh basil leaves, thinly sliced
- Cooked pasta or rice (optional)

Instructions:

1. **Drizzle** olive oil in the bottom of a 4-quart or larger slow cooker and place chicken on top. Sprinkle with salt and pepper.

2. **Stir** together tomatoes, balsamic vinegar, garlic, bay leaf, basil, and onion in a small bowl, then pour over chicken.

3. **Cook** on low until chicken reaches 155°F, about 1.5 to 2.5 hours for breasts.

4. **Transfer** chicken to a plate, cover, and let rest 5 to 10 minutes.

5. **Serve** with tomato-balsamic sauce spooned over chicken, topped with mozzarella and fresh basil.

Slow Cooker Sriracha Chili Chicken Wings

Prep Time:
15 mins

Cook Time:
2 hrs 15 mins

Servings:
4

Ingredients:

- 5 Tbsp unsalted butter
- 1/2 cup honey
- 3 Tbsp sriracha sauce
- 1 Tbsp sweet chili sauce
- 1/8 tsp kosher salt
- 3 lb chicken wings (flats/drumettes)
- Chopped cilantro
- Toasted white sesame seeds

Instructions:

1. **Melt** butter in microwave and add with honey to slow cooker.
2. **Mix** in sriracha sauce, sweet chili sauce, and salt. Add wings and toss to coat.
3. **Cook** on Low for 4-5 hours or on High for 2-3 hours.
4. **Broil** wings on a parchment-lined baking sheet for 5-8 minutes for crispy skin (optional).
5. **Garnish** with cilantro and sesame seeds if desired before serving.

Beef & Pork

Slow Cooker Pulled Pork Tacos

Prep Time:
15 mins

Cook Time:
9 hrs 15 mins

Servings:
8-10

Ingredients:

- 1 ripe pineapple
- 4 cloves garlic, grated
- 2 Tbsp olive oil, plus more for drizzling
- 1 tsp chili powder
- Roughly chopped cilantro
- 1 tsp dried oregano
- 1/2 tsp black pepper
- 1 Tbsp plus 1 tsp kosher salt, divided
- 5 lb boneless pork shoulder
- 1 medium yellow onion, thinly sliced
- 1 (7-oz) can chipotle peppers in adobo
- 1/2 cup plus 2 Tbsp distilled white vinegar, divided
- 1 1/2 Tbsp light brown sugar
- 2 small red onions, very thinly sliced
  - Flour or corn tortillas
  - 1 tsp cumin
  - Lime wedges

Instructions:

1. **Prepare** pineapple by cutting off top and bottom, peeling, coring, and slicing into rings. Reserve half for serving and chop remainder.

2. **Mix** garlic, oil, spices, and 1 Tbsp salt. Rub all over pork shoulder and place in slow cooker.

3. **Combine** chopped pineapple, yellow onion, chipotle peppers, 2 Tbsp vinegar, and water. Pour over pork with pineapple peel.

4. **Cook** on High for 6 hours or Low for 8-10 hours until pork shreds easily.

5. **Pickle** red onions with brown sugar, water, remaining salt and vinegar. Shred pork and serve with charred tortillas, caramelized pineapple rings, pickled onions, cilantro, and lime.

Slow Cooker Pulled Pork

Prep Time:
10 mins

Cook Time:
6 hrs 10 mins

Servings:
6-8

Ingredients:

- 1 5-6 lb bone-in pork shoulder roast
- 6 cloves garlic
- 4 tsp kosher salt
- 1 Tbsp brown sugar
- 2 tsp ground mustard
- 3 tsp ground black pepper
- 1 large yellow onion, thinly sliced
- 8 sprigs of thyme
- 1 cup apple cider
- 12 pretzel rolls, split and toasted
- Dijon mustard

Instructions:

1. **Trim** fat of pork shoulder to 1/4-inch thickness and cut 12 slits. Insert half a garlic clove into each slit.
2. **Combine** salt, brown sugar, mustard, and pepper. Rub all over the pork shoulder.
3. **Place** pork in slow cooker with onions, thyme, and apple cider around the sides.
4. **Cook** on High for 6 hours or Low for 8-10 hours until pull-apart tender.
5. **Serve** by pulling pork into bite-sized pieces, tossing with onions and juices, and placing on dijon-spread pretzel rolls.

Slow Cooker Pot Roast

Prep Time: 20 mins

Cook Time: 6 hrs 30 mins

Servings: 8-10

Ingredients:

- 1 whole (4-5 lb) boneless chuck roast
- 5 tsp kosher salt, divided
- 2 1/2 tsp black pepper, divided
- 4 Tbsp olive oil, divided
- 2 Tbsp tomato paste
- 1 cup beef broth
- 2 tsp Worcestershire sauce
- 6 thyme sprigs
- 3 rosemary sprigs
- 6 garlic cloves
- 1 yellow onion, cut into 1-inch wedges
- 1 lb baby yellow potatoes, halved if large
- 3 large carrots, peeled and cut into 1-inch pieces
- Drizzle of sauce from slow cooker

Instructions:

1. **Season** chuck roast with 4 teaspoons salt and 2 teaspoons pepper. Sear in oil until browned on all sides.
2. **Transfer** meat to slow cooker. Cook tomato paste in same skillet, add broth and pour over roast.
3. **Add** Worcestershire, herbs, and garlic to slow cooker. Toss vegetables with remaining oil, salt, and pepper.
4. **Arrange** vegetables around roast in slow cooker.
5. **Cook** on High for 6-8 hours or Low for 8-10 hours until fork tender. Serve with vegetables and sauce.

Slow-Cooker Drip Beef Sandwiches

Prep Time: 30 mins

Cook Time: 7 hrs 30 mins

Servings: 6

Ingredients:

- 1 (2 1/2-lb) piece beef chuck roast
- 1 tsp minced fresh rosemary
- 3/4 tsp kosher salt
- Black pepper, to taste
- 1 (12-oz) jar pepperoncini
- 1 cup beef broth
- 6 Tbsp salted butter, softened
- 1 large onion, sliced
- 6 soft hoagie rolls, split
- 12 slices provolone cheese
- Potato chips
- Extra cooking liquid for dipping

Instructions:

1. **Place** beef roast in slow cooker with rosemary, salt, pepper, pepperoncini with brine, and broth.

2. **Cook** on low for 7-8 hours until very tender. Near end, caramelize onions in butter with salt and pepper.

3. **Shred** meat and return to slow cooker. Toast buttered hoagie rolls under broiler.

4. **Assemble** sandwiches with meat, cooking liquid, pepperoncini, onions, and provolone.

5. **Broil** to melt cheese and serve with potato chips and extra cooking liquid for dipping.

Slow Cooker Brisket

Prep Time: 10 mins

Cook Time: 8 hrs 45 mins

Servings: 6

Ingredients:

- 1 (1 oz) envelope onion soup mix
- 1 Tbsp light brown sugar
- 1 1/2 tsp kosher salt
- 1/2 tsp ground black pepper
- 1 (3 lb) piece beef brisket (flat cut)
- 8 fresh thyme sprigs
- 8 whole garlic cloves
- 2 bay leaves
- 1 lb carrots, peeled and cut into 2-inch pieces
- 1 lb golden baby potatoes
- 3 celery stalks, cut into 1-inch pieces
- 1 large sweet onion, cut into 8 wedges
- 2 1/2 cups beef stock
- 2 Tbsp Worcestershire sauce
- 2 Tbsp cornstarch
- Cooking liquid gravy

Instructions:

1. **Combine** onion soup mix, brown sugar, salt, and pepper. Rub on both sides of brisket.

2. **Place** brisket fat cap down in slow cooker with herbs, garlic, and vegetables.

3. **Whisk** beef stock, Worcestershire sauce, and cornstarch. Pour into slow cooker.

4. **Cook** on High for 5-6 hours or Low for 8 hours until tender but not falling apart.

5. **Slice** brisket against the grain and serve with vegetables and gravy from slow cooker.

Slow-Cooker Teriyaki Ribs

Prep Time: 15 mins

Cook Time: 8 hrs 15 mins

Servings: 4-6

Ingredients:

- 2 racks baby back ribs (about 5 lbs total)
- 1 head garlic, cloves peeled and roughly chopped
- 1 (3-inch) piece fresh ginger, peeled and roughly chopped
- 1/2 cup honey
- 1/2 cup low-sodium soy sauce
- 1/2 cup rice vinegar
- 2 Tbsp cornstarch
- 1/4 cup mayonnaise
- 1/4 cup rice vinegar
- 2 tsp honey
- 1 lb shredded coleslaw mix
- 1 small red onion, thinly sliced
- 1 cup fresh cilantro
- Kosher salt and black pepper to taste

Instructions:

1. **Place** halved rib racks bone-side down in slow cooker over scattered garlic and ginger.
2. **Cook** on Low for 8 hours, then transfer ribs to a baking sheet and cover with foil.
3. **Prepare** sauce by straining cooking juices into a skillet, adding honey, soy sauce, and vinegar. Thicken with cornstarch slurry.
4. **Make** slaw by whisking mayonnaise, vinegar, honey, and 3 tablespoons of reserved sauce, then tossing with coleslaw mix, red onion, and cilantro.
5. **Serve** ribs coated in sauce with prepared slaw.

Slow Cooker Corned Beef and Cabbage

Prep Time: 15 mins

Cook Time: 8 hrs 15 mins

Servings: 4-6

Ingredients:

- 2 large carrots, peeled
- 1 yellow onion, peeled
- 1/2 cup grainy mustard
- 1 (3-4 lb) package corned beef brisket, with seasoning packet
- 1/2 head savoy cabbage
- 1 lb small red-skinned potatoes
- 6 sprigs fresh thyme
- 2 Tbsp honey

Instructions:

1. **Layer** carrots, onion wedges, and thyme in bottom of slow cooker, then place corned beef fat-cap side up and cover with water.
2. **Cook** on High for 5 hours after sprinkling with seasoning packet.
3. **Prepare** honey mustard by mixing mustard and honey in a small bowl.
4. **Add** cabbage wedges and potatoes around the corned beef and cook for 2 more hours.
5. **Serve** sliced corned beef with vegetables and honey mustard.

Slow Cooker Ham

Prep Time:
15 mins

Cook Time:
6 hrs 15 mins

Servings:
6-8

Ingredients:

- 1/2 cup packed light brown sugar
- 1/4 cup spicy brown mustard
- 1 Tbsp apple cider vinegar
- 1 (12-oz) can Dr Pepper or Coca-Cola
- 1 (5-7 lb) fully cooked bone-in ham
- 20 whole cloves

Instructions:

1. **Make** glaze by combining brown sugar, mustard, vinegar, and 1/2 cup soda; simmer until thick.
2. **Place** clove-studded ham in slow cooker with remaining soda and brush with 1/4 cup glaze.
3. **Cook** on Low for 5-6 hours until ham is hot throughout.
4. **Reheat** remaining glaze before ham is done.
5. **Serve** ham brushed with remaining glaze.

Drip Beef with Sherry

Prep Time: 5 mins

Cook Time: 6 hrs

Servings: 10

Ingredients:

- 1 whole (2.5-4 lb) chuck roast
- 1/4 cup butter
- 1 large onion, sliced thick
- 3 cloves garlic, peeled
- 1/2 cup soy sauce
- 1 cup sherry (cooking sherry is fine)
- 1/2 tsp salt
- 4 cups water
- Rosemary, thyme, or other spices (optional)
- Toasted, buttered deli rolls
- Cheese for broiling (optional)

Instructions:

1. **Sauté** onions in butter until starting to brown, then place chuck roast on top.
2. **Add** soy sauce, sherry, salt, water, and garlic. Cover and simmer on very low heat for 6 hours.
3. **Check** beef for tenderness, cooking longer if needed.
4. **Shred** meat with two forks until no large chunks remain.
5. **Serve** on toasted, buttered deli rolls, optionally topped with cheese and broiled.

Slow Cooker Pork Chops

Prep Time: 15 mins

Cook Time: 3 hrs 15 mins

Servings: 6-8

Ingredients:

- 1/2 cup all-purpose flour
- 1/2 tsp seasoned salt
- 1/2 tsp ground black pepper
- 1/4 tsp cayenne pepper (optional)
- 1/2 tsp chopped fresh thyme leaves, plus more for garnish
- 2 Tbsp vegetable oil
- 1 Tbsp butter
- 8 (1-inch thick) boneless pork loin chops (about 3 lbs)
- 1 large onion, sliced
- 1 (10.75 oz) can cream of mushroom soup
- 1 1/4 cups chicken broth
- 3 Tbsp Worcestershire sauce
- 4 sprigs fresh thyme
- Cooked egg noodles or mashed potatoes
- Additional fresh thyme leaves

Instructions:

1. **Dredge** pork chops in flour mixture with salt, pepper, cayenne, and thyme, then brown in oil and butter.
2. **Cook** onions in the same skillet for 5 minutes until golden.
3. **Combine** mushroom soup, broth, and Worcestershire in slow cooker, then add onions, thyme, and pork chops.
4. **Cook** on High for 1 hour, then Low for 2 more hours until pork is tender.
5. **Serve** pork chops with gravy, onions, and fresh thyme over noodles or potatoes.

Slow Cooker Hungarian Goulash & Noodles

Prep Time: 20 mins

Cook Time: 6 hrs

Servings: 6

Instructions:

1. **Coat** cubed meat with mixture of paprika, caraway seeds, marjoram, salt, flour, and pepper.

2. **Sauté** onions and garlic in olive oil, then add coated meat and brown. Add tomatoes and transfer to slow cooker.

3. **Add** broth, Worcestershire sauce, carrots, and parsnips. Cook on High for 4-5 hours or Low for 6-8 hours.

4. **Thicken** stew with cornstarch slurry during the last hour, adding sweet peppers at the same time.

5. Serve over cooked egg noodles.

Ingredients:

- 2 lbs beef chuck roast, cut into 1-inch cubes
- 1/4 cup sweet paprika
- 1 tsp caraway seeds
- 2 tsp dried marjoram
- 2 tsp kosher salt
- 1/2 tsp freshly ground black pepper
- 1 heaping Tbsp all-purpose flour
- 3 Tbsp olive oil
- 1 large yellow onion, chopped
- 3 cups beef broth
- 1 tsp minced garlic (about 2 cloves)
- 1 (14-oz) can fire-roasted diced tomatoes, undrained
- 2 Tbsp Worcestershire sauce
- 4 medium carrots, cut into 1/2-inch pieces
- 3 medium parsnips, cut into 1/2-inch pieces
- 5 oz sweet peppers, chopped
- 2 Tbsp cornstarch
- Egg noodles

Slow Cooker BBQ Pulled Beef

Prep Time:
5 mins

Cook Time:
8 hrs

Servings:
7

Ingredients:

- 2.5 lbs boneless chuck roast
- 1 Tbsp + 1/2 tsp garlic powder
- 1 Tbsp + 1/2 tsp onion powder
- 1 tsp black pepper
- 1/4 tsp crushed red pepper
- 1/2 Tbsp chili powder
- 1 1/4 tsp cumin
- 1/2 cup beef broth
- Barbecue sauce
- Hamburger buns or dinner rolls
- Salt to taste

Instructions:

1. **Season** the roast thoroughly with all dry seasonings.
2. **Add** beef broth to slow cooker, then place seasoned beef inside.
3. **Cook** on Low for 6-8 hours until tender.
4. **Shred** beef using forks or an electric mixer in a large bowl.
5. **Mix** with barbecue sauce and serve on hamburger buns or dinner rolls.

Slow Cooker Bolognese

Prep Time: 55 mins

Cook Time: 4 hrs 55 mins

Servings: 7-8 cups

Ingredients:

- 2 Tbsp olive oil, divided
- 2 celery stalks, chopped
- 1 carrot, chopped
- Kosher salt and freshly ground black pepper, to taste
- 3 cloves garlic, finely chopped
- 1/3 cup tomato paste
- 1/2 cup dry red wine
- 2 lbs ground beef
- 1 1/2 cups whole milk
- 1 (28-oz) can crushed tomatoes
- 1 1/2 tsp dried oregano
- 1 1/2 tsp dried basil
- 1 tsp dried thyme
- 1/4 tsp red pepper flakes (plus more to taste)
- 1/4 tsp ground nutmeg
- 1 parmesan rind (optional)
- 1 lb fettuccine
- Grated parmesan cheese
  - 1 onion, chopped
  - Chopped fresh basil
  - Chopped fresh parsley

Instructions:

1. **Sauté** vegetables in oil until softened, add garlic and tomato paste, then deglaze with wine.
2. **Brown** beef in same skillet, drain fat, stir in milk until absorbed, then add to slow cooker with vegetables.
3. **Add** tomatoes, herbs, spices, and parmesan rind to slow cooker and cook on High for 4 hours or Low for 6 hours.
4. **Cook** pasta according to package directions, reserving some pasta water.
5. **Serve** pasta tossed with sauce and topped with parmesan, basil, and parsley.

Red Wine Braised Short Ribs

Prep Time: 20 mins

Cook Time: 3 hrs 30 mins

Servings: 4

Ingredients:

- 4 lbs bone-in beef short ribs (English-cut)
- Kosher salt and freshly ground black pepper
- 2 tablespoons unsalted butter
- 2 tablespoons olive oil
- 1 large white onion, chopped
- 3 celery hearts, chopped
- 3 medium carrots, chopped
- 3 tablespoons all-purpose flour
- 3 tablespoons tomato paste
- 2 tablespoons Worcestershire sauce
- 2 tablespoons packed brown sugar
- 1/2 teaspoon dried oregano
- 1/2 teaspoon smoked paprika
- 1/2 teaspoon chipotle powder
- 2 cups beef broth
- 1 1/2 cups dry red wine (Merlot or Cabernet Sauvignon)
- 2 bay leaves
- Fresh herb bundle (2 sprigs each of thyme, rosemary, and sage)
- 1 head of garlic, top cut off
- Mashed potatoes or creamy polenta
- Fresh chopped herbs

Instructions:

1. **Season** short ribs with salt and pepper, then sear in butter and oil until deep brown on all sides.
2. **Sauté** vegetables until tender, add flour and tomato paste, then stir in seasonings.
3. **Return** ribs to pot, add liquids and aromatics, bring to simmer.
4. **Braise** in 325°F oven for 3-3.5 hours until meat is extremely tender.
5. **Serve** over mashed potatoes, spooning braising liquid over the top.

Slow Cooker Shepherd's Pie

Prep Time: 15 mins

Cook Time: 4 hrs 15 mins

Servings: 8

Instructions:

1. **Combine** beef cubes, vegetables, and liquid mixture in slow cooker and cook until beef is tender.

2. **Prepare** mashed potatoes separately by boiling potatoes, then mashing with milk and butter.

3. **Thicken** slow cooker mixture with flour slurry and add peas.

4. **Top** with cheese-mixed mashed potatoes.

5. **Cook** on HIGH for 15-30 more minutes until gravy thickens and potatoes are heated

Ingredients:

- 1 1/2 lbs boneless beef chuck roast, trimmed and cut into 1-inch cubes
- 3 cloves garlic, minced
- 4 medium carrots, peeled and sliced
- 8 oz white mushrooms, chopped
- 1 1/2 cups frozen corn, thawed
- 3/4 cup low-sodium beef broth
- 2 tsp Worcestershire sauce
- 1 1/2 tbsp House Seasoning
- 3 tbsp flour
- 1 tsp dried oregano
- 1 1/2 cups frozen peas, thawed
- 1 1/2 cups shredded cheddar cheese
- 6 tbsp tomato paste
- Salt and black pepper to taste
- 2 1/2 lbs russet potatoes, peeled and cut
- 1 tsp salt
- 1 cup warm milk
- 6 tbsp butter, melted
- Additional chopped herbs (optional).

Pressure Cooker Pot Roast

Prep Time: 10 mins

Cook Time: 2 hrs

Servings: 12

Ingredients:

- 1 whole beef roast (4-5 lbs)
- 2 tsp sea salt
- 1 tsp black pepper
- 1/4 cup Worcestershire sauce (or coconut aminos)
- 1 tbsp chopped fresh garlic
- 1 tsp onion powder
- 8 oz sliced mushrooms (brown or white)
- 1/2 cup beef broth
- Steamed broccoli
- Stir-fry vegetables
- Baked potatoes
- Salad ingredients

Instructions:

1. **Cut** beef roast into 4-5 large chunks and season with salt and pepper.
2. **Whisk** together Worcestershire sauce, garlic, and onion powder, then pour over beef in pressure cooker.
3. **Add** mushrooms on top and pour beef broth down the side of the pot.
4. **Cook** on high pressure for 2 hours or on low in slow cooker for 6-8 hours.
5. **Shred** meat and mix with cooking juices and mushrooms before serving.

Side Dishes & Vegetables

Crock Pot Mac and Cheese

Prep Time:
5 mins

Cook Time:
1 hr 15 mins

Servings:
8-10

Ingredients:

- 1 (16-oz) box elbow macaroni
- 2 1/2 cups whole milk
- 1 (12-oz) can evaporated milk
- 1/2 cup heavy cream
- 4 tbsp unsalted butter
- 1 tsp kosher salt
- 1/2 tsp ground black pepper
- 1/4 tsp paprika
- 1/8 tsp cayenne pepper
- 1/4 lb American cheese, cubed
- 1 (8-oz) bag shredded sharp cheddar cheese
- 1 cup shredded smoked gouda cheese
- Additional warm milk (if needed)
- Fresh chopped herbs (optional)

Instructions:

1. **Combine** macaroni, milks, cream, butter, and seasonings in a 6-8 quart slow cooker.
2. **Cook** on high for 30 minutes, stir, then cook another 25 minutes until noodles are almost tender.
3. **Add** American cheese and fold until melted, then add cheddar and gouda in batches.
4. **Serve** immediately or keep on warm setting for up to 2 hours.
5. **Stir** occasionally if holding warm, adding warm milk if sauce thickens too much.

Slow Cooker Green Beans with Bacon

Prep Time: 20 mins

Cook Time: 4 hrs 20 mins

Servings: 8-10

Ingredients:

- 8 slices thick-cut bacon, sliced 1/2-inch thick
- 1 medium yellow onion, chopped
- 3 garlic cloves, finely chopped
- 1/4 cup chicken broth
- 1 (15-oz) can diced tomatoes
- 1 (8-oz) can tomato sauce
- 2 1/2 tsp kosher salt (plus more to taste)
- 1 tsp ground black pepper
- 1/4 tsp crushed red pepper flakes
- 2 lbs fresh green beans, trimmed
- 1 1/2 tbsp red wine vinegar
- Fresh herbs (optional)
  - 1 1/2 tsp paprika
  - 1 tsp dried oregano

Instructions:

1. **Cook** bacon until crispy, transfer to paper towel-lined plate reserving drippings.
2. **Sauté** onions in bacon drippings until softened, add garlic, then deglaze with chicken broth.
3. **Transfer** mixture to slow cooker with tomatoes, sauce, seasonings, and half the bacon. Add green beans and mix.
4. **Cook** on low for 6 hours or high for 3 hours.
5. **Stir** in red wine vinegar, cook 1 more hour, and serve topped with remaining crispy bacon.

Crock Pot Stuffing

Prep Time:
20 mins

Cook Time:
2 hrs 50 mins

Servings:
8-10

Ingredients:

- 1/4 cup butter
- 3 celery stalks, chopped
- 1 yellow onion, chopped
- 1/2 tsp kosher salt
- 1/4 tsp ground black pepper
- 1 (8-oz) package sliced mushrooms
- 2 garlic cloves, chopped
- 1 (10.75-oz) can cream of mushroom soup
- 1 (14.5-oz) can chicken broth
- 1 egg
- 1 tbsp fresh parsley, chopped (plus more for serving)
- 1 tbsp fresh rosemary, chopped
- 1 tbsp fresh sage, chopped
- 1 (12-oz) bag dried bread cubes
- Cooked sausage (optional)
- Additional herbs (optional)

Instructions:

1. **Melt** butter in a skillet and cook celery, onion, salt, and pepper for 4 minutes. Add mushrooms and garlic, cook 4 more minutes.

2. **Whisk** soup, broth, egg, and herbs in slow cooker, then fold in bread cubes until coated.

3. **Add** vegetable mixture and gently fold to combine.

4. **Cook** on high for 30 minutes, then reduce to low and cook for 2 more hours without opening.

5. **Transfer** to serving bowl when center reaches 160°F or keep warm for up to 1 hour.

Crock Pot Scalloped Potatoes

Prep Time: 25 mins

Cook Time: 6 hrs 45 mins

Servings: 10-12

Ingredients:

- 5 tbsp unsalted butter, divided
- 1 small yellow onion, chopped
- 3 garlic cloves, chopped
- 1 1/2 tbsp all-purpose flour
- 2 1/2 cups heavy cream
- 2 tsp fresh thyme, chopped (plus more for garnish)
- 1 1/2 tsp black pepper
- 1 1/2 cups sharp white cheddar cheese, shredded
- 1 1/2 cups Gruyère cheese, shredded
- Freshly ground black pepper
- 4 lbs Russet potatoes (about 4 large), peeled
- Nonstick cooking spray
  - 4 tsp kosher salt
  - Additional fresh thyme

Instructions:

1. **Prepare** sauce by sautéing onions in 2 tbsp butter, adding garlic, then remaining butter and flour. Whisk in cream, seasonings, and cheeses.
2. **Slice** potatoes very thinly and layer in a greased slow cooker with cheese sauce in three alternating layers.
3. **Cook** on LOW for 6-7 hours, until potatoes are tender.
4. **Cool** for 20 minutes before serving to allow sauce to thicken.
5. **Garnish** with additional thyme and black pepper.

Slow Cooker Mashed Potatoes

Prep Time: 15 mins

Cook Time: 3 hrs 15 mins

Servings: 6

Ingredients:

- 3 lbs Russet potatoes, peeled and cut into small chunks
- 1 cup chicken broth
- 4 Tbsp unsalted butter, cut into pats
- 1 1/2 tsp salt
- 1/2 cup sour cream
- Chives or scallions, for garnish
- Heavy cream or milk, to taste (optional)

Instructions:

1. **Combine** potatoes, chicken broth, butter, and salt in slow cooker and stir together.
2. **Cook** on high for 3-4 hours, until potatoes are tender and fluffy.
3. **Mash** potatoes using a potato masher, fork, or potato ricer for smoother texture.
4. **Stir** in sour cream and add heavy cream or milk if desired.
5. **Season** to taste and garnish with chives or scallions before serving.

Slow Cooker Refried Beans

Prep Time:
10 mins

Cook Time:
12 hrs 10 mins

Servings:
8

Ingredients:

- 1 lb dried pinto beans (or kidney beans, black beans)
- 1 onion, peeled and shredded
- 4 cloves garlic, minced
- 1 Tbsp ground cumin
- 2 tsp sea salt
- 1/2 tsp cayenne pepper
- Ham bone or bacon strips (optional)
- 7 cups water
- Salt and pepper to taste
- Shredded cheese
- Sliced jalapenos
- Chopped green onions
- Sour cream
- Cayenne pepper

Instructions:

1. **Place** dried beans, shredded onion, garlic, cumin, salt, cayenne pepper, and optional ham bone or bacon in slow cooker.

2. **Pour** water over beans, cover tightly, and cook on high for 8-10 hours or on low for 12 hours.

3. **Remove** ham bone or bacon if used and reserve 1 1/2 cups of bean liquid.

4. **Mash** beans using an immersion blender or potato masher to desired consistency.

5. **Add** reserved liquid as needed and season with salt and pepper before serving with optional toppings.

Slow Cooker Garlic Herb Mushrooms

Prep Time: 10 mins

Cook Time: 2 hrs 10 mins

Servings: 6

Ingredients:

- 24 oz cremini (baby bella) mushrooms
- 4 garlic cloves, minced
- 1 tsp dried oregano
- 1 tsp dried basil
- 1/2 tsp dried thyme
- 3/4 cup vegetable broth
- Salt and pepper to taste
- 4 Tbsp unsalted butter
- Fresh parsley for garnishing

Instructions:

1. **Place** mushrooms, garlic, herbs, vegetable broth, salt, and pepper in a 4-qt slow cooker.
2. **Stir** ingredients to combine thoroughly.
3. **Cook** on HIGH for 1-2 hours or LOW for 2-3 hours, until mushrooms are tender.
4. **Add** butter during the last 15 minutes of cooking.
5. **Garnish** with chopped fresh parsley before serving.

65

Slow Cooker Southern Collard Greens

Prep Time: 20 mins

Cook Time: 6 hrs

Servings: 4-6

Ingredients:

- 3 bundles fresh collard greens
- 4 large garlic cloves, finely chopped
- 1/2 medium onion, diced
- 1 tsp kosher salt
- 1/4 tsp fresh cracked black pepper
- 1 smoked turkey wing, separated or cut in half
- 5 cups chicken stock (or 5 tsp Knorr chicken bouillon granules with 5 cups water)
- Cornbread (optional)

Instructions:

1. **Prepare** greens by removing center stems, rolling leaves, slicing into strips, and washing thoroughly.

2. **Layer** slow cooker with half smoked turkey wing, half greens, remaining turkey wing, half seasonings and onion, remaining greens, and remaining seasonings.

3. **Pour** chicken stock over the greens and cook on low for 6 hours until tender.

4. **Remove** turkey wings, shred the meat, and add back to the greens.

5. **Serve** hot, optionally with cornbread on the side.

Slow Cooker Tater Tot Casserole

Prep Time: 15 mins

Cook Time: 4 hrs 20 mins

Servings: 8

Ingredients:

- 1 Tbsp olive oil
- 1 1/2 pounds ground beef
- 1 onion, diced
- 1 (15-oz) can black beans, drained and rinsed
- 1 cup corn kernels
- 1 cup salsa
- 1 (4.5-oz) can chopped green chiles, drained
- 1 Tbsp taco seasoning mix
- 1 (10-oz) can mild enchilada sauce
- 1 (16-oz) package frozen tater tots
- 3/4 cup shredded sharp cheddar cheese
- 2 Tbsp chopped fresh cilantro leaves

Instructions:

1. **Brown** ground beef and onion in olive oil for 3-5 minutes, draining excess fat.
2. **Stir** in black beans, corn, salsa, green chiles, taco seasoning, and enchilada sauce.
3. **Layer** half the tater tots on the bottom of a greased 4-qt slow cooker, followed by the beef mixture and remaining tater tots.
4. **Cook** on low heat for 3-4 hours.
5. **Add** cheese during the last 30 minutes and garnish with cilantro before serving.

Slow Cooker Honey Glazed Carrots

Prep Time: 10 mins

Cook Time: 3 hrs 30 mins

Servings: 6-8

Ingredients:

- 2 lbs baby carrots (or regular carrots, peeled and cut into 2-inch pieces)
- 1/4 cup honey
- 3 Tbsp unsalted butter, melted
- 2 Tbsp brown sugar
- 1 tsp ground cinnamon
- 1/2 tsp ground nutmeg
- 1/2 tsp kosher salt
- 1/4 tsp black pepper
- 2 Tbsp orange juice
- 1 tsp orange zest
- 2 sprigs fresh thyme (plus more for garnish)
- 2 Tbsp fresh parsley, chopped

Instructions:

1. **Place** carrots in a 4-6 quart slow cooker.
2. **Whisk** together honey, melted butter, brown sugar, cinnamon, nutmeg, salt, pepper, orange juice, and orange zest.
3. **Pour** mixture over carrots, toss to coat, and add thyme sprigs.
4. **Cook** on LOW for 3-4 hours or HIGH for 2-3 hours, until carrots are tender but not mushy.
5. **Garnish** with fresh parsley after removing thyme sprigs and transferring to a serving dish.

Appetizers & Dips

Easy Queso Dip

Prep Time: 5 mins

Cook Time: 45 mins

Servings: 3 cups

Ingredients:

- 12 oz white American cheese
- 4 oz pepper jack cheese, shredded
- 2/3 cup half-and-half
- 1 clove garlic, chopped
- 1 jalapeño, chopped
- 1/2 tsp ground black pepper
- 4 oz green chiles, drained
- Diced tomatoes
- Chopped cilantro
- Sliced fresh jalapeño

Instructions:

1. **Combine** both cheeses, half-and-half, garlic, jalapeño, and black pepper in the slow cooker.
2. **Cook** on high for 50 minutes, stirring once halfway through.
3. **Stir** in the green chiles.
4. **Transfer** to a serving bowl or keep on warm setting.
5. **Top** with diced tomatoes, cilantro, and sliced jalapeño before serving.

Cocktail Meatballs

Prep Time: 40 mins

Cook Time: 4 hrs 40 mins

Servings: 8-10

Ingredients:

- 1 lb ground beef
- 1 lb ground pork
- 1 cup breadcrumbs
- 1/2 cup grated onion (about 1 small onion)
- 1/2 cup fresh parsley, finely chopped
- 2 large eggs
- 1 tsp kosher salt
- 1/4 tsp black pepper
- 1 12-ounce bottle chili sauce
- 1/2 cup apricot preserves
- 1 Tbsp soy sauce
- 1 Tbsp sriracha

Instructions:

1. **Combine** ground meats, breadcrumbs, onion, parsley, eggs, salt, and pepper in a large bowl and form into approximately 45 small meatballs.

2. **Whisk** together chili sauce, apricot preserves, soy sauce, and sriracha in slow cooker, reserving 1/2 cup.

3. **Arrange** meatballs in 2 layers in the sauce and pour reserved sauce over the top.

4. **Cook** on high for 4 hours, gently stirring halfway through.

5. **Serve** directly from the slow cooker or in a shallow bowl.

Crock Pot Buffalo Chicken Dip

Prep Time: 10 mins

Cook Time: 2 hrs 10 mins

Servings: 14-16

Ingredients:

- 4 cups shredded, cooked chicken (about 1 large rotisserie chicken)
- 8 oz shredded sharp cheddar cheese
- 8 oz shredded pepper jack cheese
- 2 (8-oz) packages cream cheese, softened
- 1 cup buffalo sauce (plus more for topping)
- 2/3 cup ranch dressing
- 2/3 cup blue cheese crumbles (plus more for topping)
- Chopped chives
- Carrots
- Celery sticks
- Tortilla chips

Instructions:

1. **Stir** together chicken, cheeses, cream cheese, buffalo sauce, ranch dressing, and blue cheese in a 6-quart slow cooker.
2. **Cook** on low for 2 to 4 hours, stirring occasionally.
3. **Garnish** with additional blue cheese crumbles, buffalo sauce, and chopped chives.
4. **Hold** on warm for up to 2 hours if needed.
5. **Serve** with carrots, celery sticks, and tortilla chips.

Beer Cheese Dip

Prep Time: 5 mins

Cook Time: 15 mins

Servings: 6-8

Ingredients:

- 1/4 cup unsalted butter
- 1/2 cup finely chopped yellow onion
- 1/4 cup all-purpose flour
- 1 (12-oz) can IPA beer
- 1/4 cup half-and-half
- 6 oz shredded fontina cheese
- 6 oz shredded sharp yellow cheddar cheese
- 1 tsp Dijon mustard
- 1/2 tsp Worcestershire sauce
- Chopped chives
- Black pepper
- Pretzels

Instructions:

1. **Melt** butter over medium-low heat, add onion and cook until softened, then gradually whisk in flour until lightly browned.
2. **Whisk** in beer and half-and-half, cooking until sauce thickens and just begins to bubble.
3. **Add** cheeses gradually on low heat, whisking constantly until melted and combined.
4. **Stir** in Dijon mustard and Worcestershire sauce off heat.
5. **Serve** garnished with chives and black pepper, with pretzels for dipping.

Shredded BBQ Chicken Nachos

Prep Time: 30 mins

Cook Time: 4 hrs

Servings: 8-10

Ingredients:

- 2 chicken breasts, trimmed
- 3/4 - 1 cup BBQ sauce
- 2-3 tablespoons Worcestershire sauce
- 1 teaspoon apple cider vinegar
- Salt and pepper to taste
- 2 bags (9 oz each) tortilla chips
- 1 can (15 oz) black beans, rinsed and drained
- 1 medium white onion, diced
- 1 jalapeño pepper, chopped
- 1 lb shredded cheese (sharp cheddar and Monterey Jack)
- 1/4 cup fresh cilantro, chopped
- 1 avocado, sliced
- 1/2 cup sour cream (thinned with water)
- Green onions, chopped
  - Pico de gallo
  - Hot pepper sauce

Instructions:

1. **Cook** chicken in slow cooker with BBQ sauce mixture on high for 3-4 hours, then shred and toss with sauce.
2. **Layer** tortilla chips on a baking sheet with BBQ chicken, black beans, onions, jalapeños, and cheese.
3. **Bake** at 350°F for 20-25 minutes until cheese is melted.
4. **Sprinkle** with fresh cilantro after baking.
5. **Top** with avocado, pico de gallo, sour cream, green onions, and hot sauce before serving.

Crock Pot Swedish Meatballs

Prep Time: 25 mins

Cook Time: 6 hrs

Servings: 4

Ingredients:

- 1 1/2 lbs Ground Beef (80/20)
- 1 Large Egg
- 1/2 cup Buttermilk
- 1/2 cup Breadcrumbs
- 1 tbsp Fresh Parsley, chopped
- 1 tsp Onion Powder
- 1/2 tsp Allspice
- 1/4 tsp Ground Nutmeg
- 1 tsp Black Pepper
- 1/2 tsp Kosher Salt
- 1 cup Half and Half
- 2 tbsp Cornstarch
- 1 tbsp Dijon Mustard
- 2 tsp Worcestershire Sauce
- 2 cups Beef Broth
- 4 sprigs Thyme (stems removed)
- 1 Beef Bouillon Cube
- 1 Yellow Onion, sliced
- 1 1/2 cups Portobello Mushrooms, sliced

Instructions:

1. **Prepare** meatballs by combining ground beef, breadcrumbs, parsley, seasonings, egg, and buttermilk; form into balls and broil for 6 minutes.
2. **Whisk** together half and half, cornstarch, mustard, Worcestershire sauce, beef broth, and thyme in a separate bowl.
3. **Place** meatballs in slow cooker and pour gravy mixture over them.
4. **Add** bouillon cube, onions, and mushrooms to the slow cooker.
5. **Cook** on low for 6-8 hours, stirring occasionally, and serve with mashed potatoes or noodles.

Desserts & Sweets

Crock Pot Candy

Prep Time:
5 mins

Cook Time:
1 hr 15 mins

Servings:
35-50 pieces

Ingredients:

- 2 Tbsp unsalted butter, diced
- 16 oz almond bark
- 12 oz semi-sweet chocolate chips
- 10 oz dark chocolate chips
- 10 oz peanut butter chips
- 3 cups salted, roasted peanuts
- 1 1/2 cups lightly crushed, ridged potato chips
- 1 1/2 cups crushed pretzel twists or skinny sticks
- 1 cup red and green coated candies (such as M&Ms)
- 1/4 cup sprinkles

Instructions:

1. **Place** butter in slow cooker, add chopped almond bark and all chocolate chips.
2. **Cook** on high for 30 minutes, stir, then reduce to low for 10-20 more minutes until fully melted.
3. **Stir** in peanuts, potato chips, and pretzels on warm setting.
4. **Drop** mounded scoops onto parchment-lined trays, optionally press candies on top and add sprinkles.
5. **Let** rest at room temperature until firm (30-45 mins) and store between parchment paper in refrigerator.

Slow Cooker Applesauce

Prep Time: 15 mins

Cook Time: 4 hrs 15 mins

Servings: 6

Ingredients:

- 3 lb assorted apples
- 1 cup apple juice or apple cider
- Juice of 1/2 lemon
- 1/4 cup light brown sugar
- 1/2 tsp cinnamon
- 1/2 tsp kosher salt

Instructions:

1. **Peel** the apples and cut into 1-inch chunks.
2. **Combine** all ingredients in a 4- to 6-quart slow cooker and stir.
3. **Cook** on high for 4 hours, stirring halfway through.
4. **Puree** the cooked apples using an immersion blender.
5. **Cool** before refrigerating.

Homemade Apple Butter

Prep Time: 25 mins

Cook Time: 10 hrs 25 mins

Servings: 20

Ingredients:

- 6 lbs apples (mix of Granny Smith, Fuji, and Honeycrisp)
- 1 1/2 cups brown sugar
- 2 tbsp cinnamon
- 1/2 tsp ginger
- 1/2 tsp nutmeg
- 1/2 tsp cloves
- 1 tbsp lemon juice
- 2 tbsp apple cider

Instructions:

1. **Slice** apples (peeling optional) and place in slow cooker with brown sugar, spices, lemon juice, and apple cider.
2. **Cook** on low for 10 hours, covered.
3. **Blend** until smooth and return to slow cooker on high with lid off.
4. **Mix** cornstarch and vanilla extract to create a slurry and stir into apple butter.
5. **Cook** uncovered on high for 30 minutes to 1 hour until desired thickness is reached.

Slow Cooker Banana Bread Pudding

Prep Time: 15 mins

Cook Time: 3 hrs 15 mins

Servings: 8

Ingredients:

- 6 cups day-old bread cubes (challah, brioche, or French bread)
- 4 ripe bananas, 3 mashed and 1 sliced
- 4 large eggs
- 2 cups whole milk
- 1/2 cup heavy cream
- 2/3 cup brown sugar, packed
- 1/4 cup butter, melted
- 2 tsp vanilla extract
- 1 tsp ground cinnamon
- 1/2 tsp ground nutmeg
- 1/4 tsp salt
- 1/2 cup chopped walnuts or pecans
- 1/2 cup chocolate chips (optional)
- 1/2 cup butter
- 1 cup brown sugar
  - 1/2 cup heavy cream
  - 1 tsp vanilla extract
  - Pinch of salt

Instructions:

1. **Grease** a 6-quart slow cooker and add bread cubes.
2. **Whisk** together mashed bananas, eggs, milk, cream, brown sugar, butter, vanilla, and spices in a large bowl.
3. **Pour** mixture over bread, fold in nuts and chocolate chips, and arrange banana slices on top.
4. **Cook** on LOW for 3-3.5 hours until the center is set but still moist.
5. **Prepare** caramel sauce by melting butter with brown sugar, adding cream to simmer, then stirring in vanilla and salt. Serve pudding warm with sauce drizzled on top.

Beverages

Crock Pot Hot Chocolate

Prep Time:
10 mins

Cook Time:
2 hrs 15 mins

Servings:
6-8

Ingredients:

- 1/2 cup granulated sugar
- 1/3 cup unsweetened cocoa powder
- 6 cups whole milk
- 2 cups heavy cream
- 2 (4-oz) semisweet chocolate bars, chopped
- 2 tsp vanilla extract
- 1 tsp instant espresso or coffee
- 15 marshmallows
- 8 oz Irish cream liqueur (optional)
- Additional marshmallows
- Shaved chocolate

Instructions:

1. **Whisk** sugar and cocoa powder in a 6-quart slow cooker, then gradually add milk while whisking.
2. **Add** heavy cream, chopped chocolate, vanilla extract, and instant espresso and whisk to combine.
3. **Cook** on low heat, whisking occasionally, for 2 hours.
4. **Stir** in marshmallows and cook for an additional 2 minutes until they begin to melt.
5. **Serve** with Irish cream liqueur if using, topped with additional marshmallows and shaved chocolate.

Mulled Wine

Prep Time: 5 mins

Cook Time: 35 mins

Servings: 6

Ingredients:

- 750 ml dry, fruity red wine (Merlot, Zinfandel, or Cabernet Sauvignon)
- 2 cups apple cider
- 1/4 cup honey
- 1 orange (zested and juiced)
- 5 whole cloves
- 4 green cardamom pods
- 2 cinnamon sticks
- 1 whole star anise
- 1/4 cup brandy
- Orange slices
- Cinnamon sticks

Instructions:

1. **Combine** wine, cider, honey, orange zest, and juice in slow cooker.
2. **Add** whole spices (cloves, cardamom, cinnamon sticks, and star anise).
3. **Cook** on low for 30 minutes to 1 hour (do not boil).
4. **Stir** in brandy before serving.
5. **Garnish** with orange slices and cinnamon sticks.

Homemade Slow Cooker Apple Cider

Prep Time:
10 mins

Cook Time:
3 hrs 10 mins

Servings:
12

Ingredients:

- 8 organic Gala apples, peeled and diced
- 1 large organic orange, sliced
- 8-9 cups fresh water
- 4 cinnamon sticks
- 1 tablespoon whole cloves
- 1 teaspoon ground allspice
- 1/2 cup organic brown sugar (or alternative sweetener)

Instructions:

1. **Place** apples, orange slices, cinnamon sticks, allspice, and cloves in slow cooker and cover with water.
2. **Cook** on highest setting for 3 hours until apples are completely softened.
3. **Strain** the mixture, pressing apples to extract juice, and discard solids.
4. **Stir** in brown sugar until fully dissolved.
5. **Serve** hot or chilled, optionally garnished with an orange slice and cinnamon stick.

Slow Cooker Spiced Chai Tea

Prep Time: 10 mins

Cook Time: 3 hrs

Servings: 8-10

Ingredients:

- 8 cups water
- 6 black tea bags (or 3 tablespoons loose black tea in tea infuser)
- 1 (2-inch) piece fresh ginger, sliced
- 4 cinnamon sticks
- 10 whole cardamom pods, lightly crushed
- 8 whole cloves
- 2 star anise pods
- 1/4 teaspoon black peppercorns
- 1/4 teaspoon freshly grated nutmeg
- 1/3 cup honey or maple syrup (plus more to taste)
- 2 cups whole milk or unsweetened almond milk
- 1 tablespoon vanilla extract
- Ground cinnamon
- Whipped cream (optional)

Instructions:

1. **Combine** water, ginger, cinnamon sticks, cardamom pods, cloves, star anise, peppercorns, and nutmeg in a 6-quart slow cooker.
2. **Cook** on HIGH for 1 hour to infuse the spices into the water.
3. **Add** tea bags and steep for 10 minutes, then remove them to prevent bitterness.
4. **Stir** in honey, milk, and vanilla extract, then reduce heat to LOW and cook for 2 more hours.
5. **Strain** the chai through a fine-mesh sieve into mugs and garnish with ground cinnamon and optional whipped cream.

Pasta & Casseroles

Crockpot Lasagna

Prep Time:
40 mins

Cook Time:
4 hrs 40 mins

Servings:
8

Ingredients:

- 1 pound ground beef
- 1 small yellow onion, diced
- 3 cloves garlic, minced
- 44 ounces tomato sauce
- 6 ounces tomato paste
- 1 tablespoon dried oregano
- 1 tablespoon dried basil
- 1 1/2 teaspoon kosher salt
- 1/2 teaspoon black pepper
- 1/2 teaspoon red pepper flakes
- 12 ounces lasagna noodles
- 15 ounces ricotta cheese
- 2 large eggs
- 16 ounces mozzarella cheese, shredded
- 1 cup Parmesan cheese

Instructions:

1. **Brown** ground beef with onion and garlic in a large skillet, drain excess fat, then add tomato sauce, paste, and seasonings.

2. **Reserve** 1 1/2 cups mozzarella and 1/4 cup Parmesan for topping, and mix remaining cheese with ricotta and eggs.

3. **Layer** sauce, uncooked lasagna noodles (broken to fit), and cheese mixture in a greased 6-8 quart slow cooker.

4. **Repeat** layers until ingredients are used up, then top with reserved cheese.

5. **Cook** on low for 4-6 hours until bubbly and cooked through.

Slow Cooker Mexican Lasagna

Prep Time: 15 mins

Cook Time: 3 hrs

Servings: 6

Instructions:

1. **Cook** garlic and onions in olive oil until soft, then add ground turkey with seasonings and lime juice. Stir in cilantro when turkey is cooked.

2. **Layer** ingredients in slow cooker: enchilada sauce, corn tortillas, beans, corn, tomatoes, chiles, turkey, and cheese. Repeat layers two more times.

3. **Cover** and cook on high for 2 1/2 hours, until cheese is melted and lasagna is bubbling.

4. **Serve** with suggested toppings like diced tomatoes, avocados, radishes, cilantro, and sour cream.

5. **Store** leftovers in refrigerator for up to 4 days or freeze for longer storage.

Ingredients:

- 1 tablespoon olive oil
- 1 tablespoon minced garlic
- 1 medium onion, chopped
- 1 pound ground turkey
- 1 teaspoon ground cumin
- 1 teaspoon chili powder
- 1/2 teaspoon dried oregano
- Salt and black pepper to taste
- Juice of 1 lime
- 1/4 cup chopped cilantro
- 2 1/2 cups red enchilada sauce
- 6 corn tortillas
- 1 (15-oz) can black beans
- 1 (15-oz) can corn
- 1 (15-oz) can diced tomatoes, drained
- 2 (4-oz) cans diced green chiles
- 1 1/2 cups shredded Mexican cheese
- Diced tomatoes
- Avocados
- Radishes
- Cilantro
- Sour cream

Measurement Conversion Chart

Volume Conversions

US Customary	Metric
1/4 teaspoon	1.25 ml
1/2 teaspoon	2.5 ml
3/4 teaspoon	3.75 ml
1 teaspoon	5 ml
1 tablespoon	15 ml
1/4 cup	60 ml
1/3 cup	80 ml
1/2 cup	120 ml
2/3 cup	160 ml
3/4 cup	180 ml
1 cup	240 ml
1 pint	470 ml
1 quart	950 ml
1 gallon	3.8 liters

Temperature Conversions

Fahrenheit	Celsius
32°F	0°C
140°F	60°C
160°F	71°C
180°F	82°C
200°F	93°C
225°F	107°C
250°F	121°C
275°F	135°C
300°F	149°C
325°F	163°C
350°F	177°C
375°F	191°C
400°F	204°C
425°F	218°C
450°F	232°C

Weight Conversions

US Customary	Metric
1/2 ounce	15 g
1 ounce	28 g
2 ounces	57 g
4 ounces	113 g
8 ounces	227 g
12 ounces	340 g
16 ounces (1 pound)	454 g
2 pounds	907 g
4 pounds	1.8 kg

Common Ingredient Conversions

Ingredient	Volume	Weight
All-purpose flour	1 cup	125 g
Granulated sugar	1 cup	200 g
Brown sugar (packed)	1 cup	220 g
Confectioners' sugar	1 cup	120 g
Butter	1 cup	227 g
Vegetable oil	1 cup	224 g
Rice (uncooked)	1 cup	185 g
Rolled oats	1 cup	90 g

Thank you for your purchase!

We've prepared a special bonus pack just for you — filled with helpful tools and resources:

⇨ Weekly Meal Planner
⇨ Shopping List Template
⇨ Cooking Setup Checklist
⇨ Wellbeing Tracker

Simply scan the QR code below to access your bonuses or get any help along the way.

Wishing you many delicious moments!

Printed in Dunstable, United Kingdom